Keeping a personal–professional journal

Mary Louise Holly
Kent State University

Peter Klehher

Birchip

September 1994

Deakin University
Victoria 3217

Published by Deakin University, Victoria 3217
Distributed by Deakin University Press
First published 1984
Revised Edition 1987
Reprinted 1985, 1987, 1991, 1992

Edited and designed by Deakin University Production Unit
Printed by Brown Prior Anderson Pty Ltd Burwood Victoria

National Library of Australia
Cataloguing-in-publication data

Holly, Mary Louise, 1946– .
    Keeping a personal–professional journal.

    Bibliography.
    ESA 843.
    ISBN 0 7300 0145 8.

    1. Teachers — In-service training. I. Deakin University. School
    of Education. Open Campus Program. II. Title. III. Title:
    School-based professional development.

371.1'46

This book forms part of the **ESA843 School-based professional
development** course offered by the School of Education in
Deakin University's Open Campus Program.

Course team
B. T. Dickie
C. E. Henry
D. Macmillan (course developer)
W. J. Smyth (course team chairperson)

Consultants
M. L. Holly
N. Garman

The **ESA843 School-based professional development** course
includes:
M. L. Holly, *Keeping a Personal–Professional Journal*
W. J. Smyth, *Clinical Supervision—Collaborative Learning about
    Teaching: A Handbook*
W. J. Smyth (ed.), *Case Studies in Clinical Supervision*
ESA843 *School-Based Professional Development: Course Guide and
    Readings*

These books are available from Deakin University Press, Deakin
University, Victoria 3217.

Acknowledgements
We should like to thank all those authors, publishers and other
copyright holders who kindly gave us permission to reproduce
material in this book. While every care has been taken to trace
and acknowledge copyright, we tender our apologies for any
accidental infringement. We should be pleased to come to a
suitable arrangement with the rightful owner in such a case.

Foreword

Actually making sense of teaching experiences to learn and gain from them is easier said than done. The obvious good sense of actively reflecting upon events and occurrences belies the practical difficulties involved. As adults involved in the reality of crowded and hurried classroom and administrative schedules, we tend to overlook the need for 'private space' in which to explore and extract meaning from what we do. Rather than exercising a measure of control over our professional lives, we become so enmeshed in our own circumstances that we are unwittingly swept along by the complex tide of events.

What this book does in a concise and readable way is provide a rationale for distancing ourselves from the press of daily occurrences so we can locate ourselves in the stream of events that represents our unique reality. Through her discussion of the potential benefits of writing about teaching and collegial interaction, by looking at the experiences of those who have used writing as a way of collecting and analysing experiences, and by providing concrete guidelines on how to proceed with a journal, Mary Lou Holly has provided teachers with a way of reflecting upon practice in order to appreciate it and then change it, if necessary.

Course team chairperson

Special acknowledgements

I would like to acknowledge Judy, Carole, Jerry, Craig, Marcia, and Kate—teachers who shared their insights into journal writing; Helen Hulbert, John Smyth, Richard Hawthorne, Roy Edelfelt, Brian Holly, Jane Applegate, and Sandy Gustafson for their assistance and suggestions; and Bonnie Heaton for her patience and deft typing.

The development of ideas for this monograph and the teacher portraits included in it are the result of a research project supported in part under Grant Number NIE-G-81-0014 from the National Institute of Education, Research and Practice Unit, Knowledge Use and School Improvement. Any opinions and conclusions expressed herein represent those of the author and not necessarily those of the agency.

Contents

Part 3: Journal keeping—a writer's manual

Introduction

There are no hard and fast rules for journal keeping. Each of us must develop procedures and organisation according to our style and purposes. This paper provides a context for journal writing, and some suggestions and ideas, which were formulated from my journal keeping over the past several years and from my work with practising teachers who have kept journals and diaries.

A journal is a personal document. The writer is usually the only one to read it. The journal excerpts in this paper come mainly from schoolteachers who kept diaries/journals (the differences between diaries and journals will be addressed shortly) as part of a year-long research project on teaching and professional development (Holly 1983a, 1983b; for an abstract of this project, see Appendix). They shared their journals with me and excerpts with each other throughout the project. The teachers were asked to reflect on each day, and to note meaningful recollections. The content, style, and organisation, as well as when and where they wrote, were matters of personal choice. Because we went about writing in a non-directed way, we learned many lessons in journal keeping—some, the hard way.

This monograph is organised into three parts. Part 1 starts with an overview of journal keeping. After looking at three forms of written personal documentation—the log, the diary, and the journal—we briefly mention some of the people who have used these processes. This section concludes by describing several facets of the writing process. In Part 2, journal writing is considered as a tool for professional development. Three case studies of teachers and their experiences as they engaged in reflective writing are presented from my own research. Part 3 contains information and suggestions on several practical matters for journal keeping, such as: how to begin keeping a journal, what to write about, and some ways to learn from writing. A list of articles and books about writing and journal keeping is also included in the 'Recommended reading' list.

Part 1: Journal keeping

The journal

Introduction

I'd rather learn from one bird how to sing than to teach ten thousand stars how not to dance.

E. E. CUMMINGS

Keeping a journal is a humbling process. You rely on your senses, your impressions, and you purposely record your experiences as vividly, as playfully, and as creatively as you can. It is a learning process in which you are both the learner and the one who teaches.

A journal is not merely a flow of impressions, it is impressions plus descriptions of circumstances, others, the self, motives, thoughts, and feelings. Taken further, it can be used as a tool for analysis and introspection. It is a chronicle of events as they happen, a dialogue with the facts (objective) and interpretations (subjective), and perhaps most important, it is an awareness of the difference between facts and interpretations. A journal becomes a dialogue with oneself, over time. To review journal entries is to return to events and their interpretation with the perspective of time. Over time, patterns and relationships emerge that were previously isolated events 'just lived'. Time provides perspective and momentum, and enables deeper levels of insight to take place.

Logs, diaries, and journals

Personal documents have been written since the beginning of written language. In fact, recorded history is in many ways a journal—someone's impressions, thoughts, ideas, and not as obviously someone's feelings about events. There are basically three types of personal documentation: logs, diaries, and journals. Often books, historical and literary, are reconstructed accounts from such documents.

Logs

The ship's log is probably the most recognised type of log. The term originally referred to a bulky piece of unshaped lumber that was used to measure the ship's motion and speed through the water. Knowing how fast the ship's engines were running was only part of computing the progress of the ship—currents and winds were also important determinants. Actual speed was established via the log. Log books were the official records of the ship's voyage: speeds, distances, wind speeds, direction travelled, fuel used, weather, and other navigational facts. Normal and unusual happenings were recorded for each 24-hour period. Though the log books were kept in formal sober language, dramatic stories of casualties and emergencies are implicit in the logs. Courts of law accept log entries as evidence, and during wartime, commanders of naval vessels use log books to record their operations and progress. Events and circumstances at sea can then be reconstructed by historians.

The log is used now to refer to 'a regularly kept record of performance' (*Merriam-Webster Dictionary* 1974) and is used by social scientists, writers, airline pilots, teachers, and others to record certain types of information. Just as the ship's log was a description of conditions and happenings, today's log is a recording of facts pertaining to specific occurrences. Some teachers find it useful, for example, to keep a log on an individual child's behaviour and progress in school. In this way, they can begin to see patterns in the learning style of the child. Only after keeping the log over a period of time do key patterns become clear. When teachers go over their lesson-plan books and record what they actually do during the week, they are keeping a log of the class's curricular progress.

Diaries

While logs are concerned predominantly with factual information (most recorders in logs would agree on what happened, i.e. the speed of the ship; the stories completed in literature class; interruptions, whether a sudden wind or intercom announcement), diaries are usually a more personal and interpretive form of writing. Diaries are often less structured in the form that experiences are included and depicted. The way events are described is often dictated by the writer's thoughts and feelings about them: factual information is included in a way that supports the writer's perspective at the time. There is less concern for 'objectivity' and more attention to the way the experiences felt. In many diaries there is a 'let it out' nature, a capturing of impressions lived, rather than a careful documentation and thoughtful reconstruction of events and circumstances. Depending on the purposes and moods of the writer, diary entries can be factual, emotional, thoughtful, or impressionistic.

In general, diaries are open ended: anything that can be verbalised can be included. At times, the writer has a specific topic in mind to write about; at other times, thoughts flow unrestrictedly onto the page. The degree of structure framing the writing depends entirely on the writer, whereas in a log, some structure is usually planned beforehand. Diary entries can be as structured as those of a log, though log entries are rarely as free flowing as diary entries. In a log, the writer's feelings about the events he or she is describing are of little or no value to the reader, and in fact, inclusion of the writer's thoughts and feelings can call into question the objectivity of the recording.

Because diary writing is interpretive, descriptive on multiple dimensions, unstructured, sometimes factual, and often all of these, it is difficult to analyse. It is not easy to separate thoughts from feelings from facts and, as the writer, to extricate yourself from your writing. This is not true of the log, which is often written with other readers in mind. The diary doesn't judge or offer interpretation. There is less opportunity for multiple perspectives though, since few of us let others read our diaries. But because they are personal, even if others do read our diaries, their 'help' may not be so helpful. Few of us have friends who are willing or perhaps even capable of poring over our personal statements and questions for any length of time.

These seeming constraints—the open nature of entries, and the personal interpretations we lend to them—are also sources of the diary's potential use and strength. Who helps us 'absorb' (Liske, personal communication, 1982) those aspects of our teaching days that we must? Who listens with a quiet heart (nonjudgementally) to our thoughts and feelings about what we see and hear, what we do and what happens to us as teachers? What do we do to remove ourselves from the motion of, the action of, teaching? In what ways do we enable ourselves to reflect on our lives as teachers? Recording in our diaries allows us to do these things. It removes us from the motion of doing and transports us to the reflective act of pondering on paper, while at the same time, it captures some of the action of teaching to come back to with the perspective that time brings.

Journals

Journal writing can include the structured, descriptive, and objective notes of the log and the free-flowing impressionistic meanderings of the diary. That is, it can serve the purposes of both logs and diaries. It is a more difficult and perhaps more demanding document to keep—indeed, it is more complex. Its advantages are also greater: it combines purposes and it extends into other uses. The contents of a journal are more comprehensive than those of either a log or a diary. It is a reconstruction of experience and, like the diary, has both objective and subjective dimensions, but unlike most diaries, there is a consciousness of this differentiation.

In a journal, the writer can carry on a dialogue between and among various dimensions of experience. What happened? What are the facts? What was my role? What feelings and senses surrounded events? What did I do? What did I feel about what I did? Why? What was the setting? The flow of events? And later, what were the important elements of the event? What preceded it? Followed it? What might I be aware of if the situation recurs? This dialogue, traversing back and forth between objective and subjective views, allows the writer to become increasingly more accepting and perhaps less judgemental as the flow of events takes form. Independent actions take on added meaning.

A **research journal** (or section of a journal) is a tool for focusing on a specific topic. Many researchers keep detailed journals of their research. They document their ideas and collect data, or evidence, along the way. They use their journal as documentation for both formative (throughout the project) and summative (at the conclusion of the project) analysis and evaluation. Important considerations in keeping a research journal are to keep comprehensive, descriptive documentation, to record procedures and interactions (including verbal information), and to keep analytical and interpretive notes. The analytical and interpretive notes should be recognised as such, for they should lead to reconstruction of the project from objective and subjective dimensions. The research, your purposes and procedures will, of course, dictate the content and methods of writing in the research journal.

Writing to reflect

Writing to reflect involves a cyclical pattern of reflection: first, reflecting on experiences before or as you write; and then, reflecting on the journal entries themselves at some later stage, which may provide material for further reflection and writing, and so on.

Many of us find it difficult, even painful, to return to diary and journal writing after the event. Perhaps part of the reason is because we see our emotions and relive our experiences, often without the benefit of the context within which those events took place. We may wonder how we could have been so distressed over seemingly trivial events, but when given the flow of circumstances, our behaviour seems natural. It is the piecing together of the flow that enables acceptance and *then* analysis and change, as a result of changes in perception. In my experience, once I see a more holistic or comprehensive picture, the tendency to become defensive, to ward off dissonance between my image of myself and my behaviour, diminishes. I interpret the world through my perceptions, which are influenced by my motivations. If I see only the facts of a situation, or I reflect only on my thoughts and feelings about it, it is easy for me to close off the very interactive aspects of the situation that might enable me to understand it. My thoughts close off before I have enough evidence to explore my experiences.

The tendency to judge—to dichotomise good and bad, success and failure—seems to be strongest when the complexity of our circumstances outstrips our ability to understand them. We simplify our experiences until later when we can view them less defensively and more comprehensively. But, in a time of rapid technological change and an emphasis on 'higher productivity', it becomes hard to differentiate what *is* important from what *is not* important. And perhaps the more hurried we are, the less likely is reflection and the more likely 'stress' or 'burnout' and closed-off perceptions.

Taking time out for reflective writing and dialogue is an attractive alternative to running at our current speed or speeding up and 'burning out'. Through the journal-keeping process, we can become more sensitive observers, more penetrating in our inquiry into 'what it all means', and more focused on our roles and directions in life.

According to Progoff (1975), there are two ways to record in a log, diary, or journal: (1) write close to the time of experiences; or (2) reflect back over the day or few days, as soon as possible, perhaps early in the morning or at night in the quiet—or you can do both, by jotting down ideas in snatches as they occur to you and expanding on them later. You might wish to record key words or phrases for later expansion. Writing soon after the experience is sometimes preferable, though not always possible. And sometimes it is harder to 'selectively remember' our experiences the closer we are to them; on these occasions, it is easier to recall events more comprehensively with the distance of time. So we might use a combination of writing as close to the time as possible *and* some time later so that multiple views could emerge.

A quiet place is desirable for keeping a log or diary. The journal writer needs to reflect quietly, to go back and reconstruct or recapture the setting, thoughts, and feelings at the time—the flow of events. Once these flows are felt, other events, behaviours, or ideas that 'fit' with them will become increasingly evident. The journal holds experiences as a puzzle frame holds its integral pieces. The writer begins to recognise the pieces that fit together and, like a detective, sees the picture evolve. Clues lead to new clues, partial perspectives to holistic perspectives.

Writing to clarify

Many prominent philosophers, artists, writers, and statespeople have kept diaries or journals, some admittedly as a reflective process. We are afforded glimpses of history, of the tragedy, comedy, and fundamental dilemmas of life through the diaries and journals of people like Samuel Pepys (1893), Anne Frank (1952), Virginia Woolf (1953), and Dag Hammarskjold (1964).

Providing the first systematically recorded insights into child development in 1601, Heroard (Papalia & Olds 1975) began a diary on the heir to the French throne, the child of Henry IV. Then, Charles Darwin (1877) and Jean Piaget (1952) provided further insights into child growth and development while Abraham Maslow (1979) and Ira Progoff (1975) illustrate adult growth through journal writing. Rudyard Kipling (1930), Charles Dickens (1917), and Miles Franklin (1901) used their autobiographical writing to develop realistic portraits of their times. Sylvia Ashton-Warner (1973) documents, from a teacher's point of view, the challenges she faced.

All of these people recorded aspects of their lives that were important to them at the time. For each of them, personal writing is, or was, a way of clarifying their perceptions, thoughts, and feelings. It led to growth in their ideas and to important contributions to their fields.

An interesting characteristic of most of these diary/journal writers is their apparently nonchalant attitude toward their own lives. They are interested in recording their ideas, but they rarely approach the content of their writing as if it were extraordinary. Yet, as they write of their experiences, they seem to be much more aware of life as it unfolds than the rest of us. (A surprising thing happens to many of us though, as we keep journals: we find we become more aware of our surroundings and experiences than we did before we wrote.) Miles Franklin's first book, *My Brilliant Career*, based on her experiences as an outspoken adolescent living in a small Australian bush community, and published in 1901, when she was 21, illustrates this well.

The writing process

The joy of the ride, even more than the arrival, is the motive force behind the artist's work.

(E. W. EISNER, *The Educational Imagination*, p. x.)

Writing well is an artistic process. While few of us consider ourselves artists with the written word, we can profitably and happily write to stroll, meander, backtrack, jog, and dash out our experiences, as well as our dreams. Writing is a form of personal expression that is directed by a sense of aesthetic balance: a creative tension between the inner self and the outer world expressed in words, a personal story constructed by the author.

Verbal and written expression

Whether we write or speak, we use words. Yet, these two modes of presentation differ in many ways. Verbal expression uses clues like facial and body expression, tone of voice, cadence, time, syntax, and volume to convey messages; the written word depends largely on itself to seek images. Whereas the spoken word often disappears in the air waves that produce it, the written word, like a painting, remains. Both verbal and written expression convey thoughts and feelings, and usually leave us with a sense of what we think the author meant, but in a verbal exchange, we can clarify our thoughts by asking questions of those with whom we are communicating. Misunderstandings or misinterpretations can be cleared up through the process of questions answered. When communicating with the written word, clarity must be established by the words we place on paper. As a result, writing may take longer, and the words will likely be fewer and more to the point. Like children learning to speak using telegraphic speech (using only the most important words), the writer sifts out words that may not be necessary.

Speaking is faster than writing. It often suffers the risk of less attention to selection of words, syntax, grammar, or enunciation. We may convey thoughts as they come to us with as much variation and enthusiasm as we feel, recognised or not. We often speak impetuously, without thinking, remembering selectively. The written word, in contrast, is usually more deliberate. We 'picture' what we want to say on paper and edit as, and after, we write. However, writing can also flow quickly and provide us with time to ponder our experience after our words are written. We can examine them carefully, and then express ourselves less impetuously.

Partly because writing provides more time for reflection, it can be more frustrating than speaking. Translating images to verbal messages, using body language and other visual clues seems more natural than translating these same images into the written word, where 'it all must be there—on paper' (R. A. Edelfelt, personal communication, 1982). We become aware of our grammar and of writing in complete sentences at the same time as we are concerned with conveying ideas and images as we see and feel them. We are more aware of our inadequacies in selecting words as purveyors of meaning. It is difficult to portray the excitement and intensity of our experiences. Our feelings are similar to those of the fifth-year or sixth-year primary school children who lose enthusiasm for drawing because they cannot portray the 'reality' they see. Unlike log writing, diary and journal writing is often more spontaneous and less deliberate than writing designed to communicate to others—in fact, if it becomes too deliberate, it can restrict the expression of feeling and impressions. When this happens, we become more preoccupied with *how* we say something and less concerned with saying *what* we feel and think (R. Edelfelt, personal communication, 1983).

People's writing and speaking styles are sometimes very different (W. J. Smyth, personal communication, 1983). Some of us find it difficult to speak articulately, but find that writing conveys our ideas quite well, while those who are verbally facile sometimes find their writing awkward and distant, if not distorted, from the intended messages.

Regardless of whether we use oral or written communication, reflection can lead to increased understanding and increased awareness of the self and others; it can also (and often does) lead to rationalisation and distortion of experiences. The question is, how does one 'capture' the moment and also reflect upon it later with validity? (R. Hawthorne, personal communication, 1983). In a sense, the further we are from our experiences, the more time there is for both distortion and increased understanding. Which one dominates is a product of the circumstances and our relationship to them. However, if we record some of our verbalisations and bring into awareness some of our unconscious thoughts and feelings, we have the opportunity of returning to them to see whether they hold up over time.

Writing to explore
Introduction

Writing does more than convey our pictures of events and feelings: through it we can describe, analyse, and clarify events—those on a conscious level and those only dimly sensed.

The act of writing may lead to further reflecting on, and reconstructing of, experiences; reliving in our mind can deepen awareness, broaden perspective, and increase understanding of experience. A later look can provide a perspective from outside the situational context and permit examination of the context and factors that influence it. Perspective writing (writing with the perspective of time) can enable us to confirm, explain, expand, or change ideas/insights gained in a second or third reflection. These potential benefits take time and they are by no means inevitable. For these reasons, writing can be an uncomfortable process.

While each of us seeks to grow and change, we also find it difficult to give up the comfort and security of our current perceptions. Returning to descriptions of our thoughts, feelings, and actions is both gratifying and disconcerting, depending on what we wrote and how we interpret it at a later time. Often we write with the feeling or assumption that there will be a reader (though we have no conscious intention of sharing our writing) and that though there is a willingness to 'tell all', to bare our soul and feelings, there remains the ego, the self-concept, and the need to demonstrate personal legitimacy. (R. A. Edefelt, personal communication, 1983). Writing descriptively is for most of us an enjoyable, if challenging, endeavour. Writing reflectively and introspectively takes a bit more self-confidence.

Exploring experience

There are many different types of writing. The novelist writes in a different way than does the journalist, the chemist different than the therapist, the anthropologist different than the poet, and one poet different from another. To explore our experiences through journal writing, we can draw from many different types of writing. Which one is appropriate to use at a certain time will be determined by our purposes at the time we write. Comments on five types of writing will be presented: journalistic, analytical, ethnographic, creative-therapeutic, and introspective.

Journalistic writing. A journalist describes events and circumstances surrounding the news to be reported. Factual information is presented as the journalist describes relevant aspects of the topic. A journalist views the circumstances as an outsider-observer. When facts are interpreted, it is usually made obvious to the reader that these are interpretations.

Analytical writing. When writing analytically, attention is directed to component parts, or constituent elements, of the topic. The analytical writer studies the nature of the parts and the relationships of one part to another, and the subject is broken down into smaller parts for analysis. This type of writing is a form of thinking and reasoning. Each important element can be inspected and described.

Ethnographic writing. This type of writing is grounded in the observer's observations and experience. Ethnographic writing is used by ethnographers (descriptive anthropologists) and others to describe people within their specific social and cultural contexts. It can be phenomenological, comparative, and analytical, as the researcher seeks to capture important elements of the person within their context. When beginning an ethnographic observation, the writer often becomes immersed in the setting and tries to become a participant and an observer. Because different aspects of study are important from different perspectives, the researcher starts by keeping detailed observation (or field) notes that enable a comprehensive reconstruction of the observed setting and events. In this way patterns can *emerge from the data*, whereas in other types of study the researcher narrows the focus before observing.

Creative-therapeutic writing. Though creative-therapeutic writing can be a slow and thoughtful process, like other types of writing, its unifying and unique characteristic is its tapping of our inner selves in what can be a free-flowing, spontaneous nature; the writer lets the words flow onto the paper without attention to 'how they sound'. Sometimes complete sentences unfold; at other times, images and poetic phrases. Creative-therapeutic writing is sometimes done at the height of feeling; it can be expanded and edited during times of calm; it can evolve in times of both quiet and chaos. This type of writing is rarely devoid of feeling and can at times be quite uncomfortable, while at other times (or in concert with this feeling of discomfort), a great feeling of exhilaration and well-being accompanies or follows it. 'Just writing makes me feel better' and 'I had to stop writing; I was going too deep' are two sides of this type of writing. 'I didn't know I felt this way.' 'I like the way these words sound.' Creative-therapeutic writing introduces us to ourselves, and makes known to us concerns and interests previously unknown on a conscious level.

Introspective writing. For many of us, this is the most challenging and disconcerting type of writing. It is the examination of our own thoughts, sensory experiences, feelings, and behaviour. There are many reasons for our behaviour, but we rarely step back to ask ourselves, 'Why did I do/feel/think that?'. Habit, motivation, and sometimes our own biases and unrecognised needs move us to behave in ways that are uncomfortable when we question ourselves. We allow ourselves to be vulnerable when we question ourselves. Our humanness shows. We sometimes feel threatened by change and the discomfort that accompanies the cognitive dissonance arising from the difference between our image of ourselves and our behaviour. To write introspectively means to march, if slowly at times, through barriers to discover the motives and circumstances that influence our behaviour. To write reflectively means to write thoughtfully, deliberately, and considerately.

Journal writing usually includes aspects of all these types of writing. Each will introduce us to different dimensions of, and perspectives on, our experience. We can become more appreciative and accepting of ourselves, and less judgemental. We can learn from our experiences, but only if we appreciate them. The Pilgrims, for example, used lobster for fertiliser! Like the Pilgrims, we have many resources lurking throughout our days that might lead to an improvement in the quality of our lives (and promote professional growth); we have only to recognise and use them.

Writing is an antidote to the anaesthetic that slowly beclouds us as we step into routines to protect ourselves from the many demands of teaching. Greene (1982, p. 3) points out that 'persons must be aroused to self-reflectiveness; they must be moved to search'. She illustrates this by reference to the narrator in Walker Percy's (1980) *The Moviegoer*, who 'decides that everything is upside down; and he stumbles on the idea of the search' (Greene 1982, pp. 3–4):

> This morning, for the first time in years, there occurred to me the possibility of a search . . .
>
> What is the nature of the search? you ask.
>
> Really, it is very simple, at least for a fellow like me; so simple that it is easily overlooked.
>
> The search is what anyone would undertake if he were not sunk in the every-dayness of his own life. This morning, for example, I felt as if I had come to myself on a strange island. And what does such a castaway do? Why he pokes around the neighbourhood and he doesn't miss a trick.
>
> To become aware of the possibility of the search is to be onto something. Not to be onto something is to be in despair.

(Percy 1980, p. 18)

Part 2: Journal keeping for professional development

Professional development

... into his fateful heap of days and deeds
the soul of man is cast.

EDWIN MARKHAM, 'A Creed'

Introduction

David Elkind (1981), noted child psychologist, has called our attention to 'the hurried child'. Who hurries children? We, hurried adults, do. Dwindling economic support, rising 'standards', employment instability, changing family structures, population shifts, and concomitantly fewer new teachers joining the profession each year—*each* contributes to 'developing downward': that is, the reverse of the growth in schools and program development of the late 1960s and 1970s. Thus, we find 'accountability', 'burnout', and 'teacher stress' are associated with teaching today, and each of these serves to frame the way in which we treat our children.

In a time of burgeoning technology, we as educators are often caught up in teaching 'more', 'sooner', and 'faster'. Parents are concerned that their children acquire the educational experiences that will enable them to succeed; administrators must co-ordinate, manage, and provide leadership skills to promote curricular, professional, and staff development with fewer people and dwindling resources (people, services, and money). As teachers, we are becoming increasingly aware that we cannot solve many of our children's, or any of society's, problems, and that teaching is far more complex than our 'methods of teaching' courses lead us to believe. The kind of 'instruction' that makes a significant difference to the lives of children is more likely when the children we teach are ready, willing, and able; when our roles of decision maker, interactor, learner-scholar, colleague, and member of the profession are balanced and complementary; and when the climate and conditions of the environment under which we teach are supportive of our efforts. As important as these conditions are, they only assist us in the process of orchestrating our ideas, theories, values, attitudes, and knowledge with the children and youth in our classrooms.

Today we have the opportunity to improve education. We have stability in the teaching profession. Teachers are staying where they are. The public shows signs of concern and readiness to support education; classrooms are being viewed as professionally respected places where there is the realisation of professional competence and experience. Rather than subjects for scrutiny and prescriptions, classrooms have become arenas for description. How do teachers teach? Why do teachers do what they do? How do they think and feel about teaching? How do they balance individual and group development? How do they walk back and forth between the content and processes of teaching? How do they manage the complexity of teaching 30 children six hours a day, five days a week, for 180 days a year? What are their dilemmas? Their joys and satisfactions? Frustrations? How do teachers grow and learn?

Educational researchers no longer labour under the assumption that what they see in the classroom is the 'whole story' of teaching. In the book *Beyond Surface Curriculum*, Bussis et al. (1975) document teachers 'constructs', the ideas and philosophies behind their work. It has become clear through their research and other studies that educational improvement will only come about as teachers develop professionally, and that telling teachers how to improve is not the answer. We've only just begun to ask, 'What *do* teachers do?' and 'Why?'. So 'answers' are a bit more complicated and situation specific than previous attempts at prescription might suggest.

These last two questions look so simple: What *do* teachers do? Why? Yet responding to them is difficult. Have you ever posed these questions to yourself? As Craig, a kindergarten teacher, said, 'these are the most difficult questions you can pose to a teacher'. He finds that he is so busy teaching and taking care of administrative tasks related to the classroom that he rarely has time to reflect on what he does and why. As he began to reflect on his teaching day in order to write about significant aspects of it, he found that he'd never *really* thought about much of his behaviour in the classroom. It was easy to think about the children individually, about their behaviour and progress, but it was very difficult to think about his own behaviour. Craig began to protect time regularly for reflecting and writing. He looks back on his six years of teaching and wonders why these questions didn't come up before. 'How can we [teachers] teach without seriously thinking about it?'

Keeping a journal is a way to ponder these questions, and others. It is a way to document what you do, events that hold significance for you as a teacher, and to clarify your beliefs and assumptions, and further, to test these out in your behaviour. As you write about what happens in the classroom, what you do, and how you think and feel about both your children's and your own experiences, you will begin to see where your philosophy and 'theories' are demonstrated in your behaviour and where they are in conflict with them. You will be able to work out some of your dilemmas as you 'think on paper' about them. You will find patterns and behaviours that you were not aware of before. You will at times be pleased; other times you will find things you would like to change. Merely by calling attention to these 'hidden' facets of your teaching, you will be informing your practice. Like Craig, you might find yourself quite comfortable when asked 'Why did you do that?'. And, even more importantly, you might find yourself becoming comfortable with ambiguity, complexity, and the unsettling nature of continuous inquiry.

In the 5th Century BC, Socrates suggested that 'the life which is unexamined is not worth living'. Today, the push to teach 'more', 'sooner' and 'faster' exerts pressure for movement and action. However, if our efforts are to be consistent with our aims, we must also examine our aims. Keeping a journal is a way to help us do just that. We capture events to which we can return later to sift unhurriedly through from a different perspective. We live in a time of 'quick fixes', but if we want the fix to work, it must fit the circumstances. Keeping a journal is a way to help us see the circumstances, to document experiences over time so that we can see the flow of events rather than isolated instances.

Adult development and teacher growth

Psychologists since Freud have focused on child development. Relatively recently, many psychologists have taken an interest in adult development and education to promote the development of teachers. Much of their research is encouraging as they continue to document significant development, learning, and growth throughout the life cycle. In particular, the work of Knowles (1978), Hunt (1978), and Sprinthall & Sprinthall (1980, 1983) offers insights into teacher growth that are consistent with reflective writing.

According to Knowles, for example, as adults, our orientation to learning is life-centred. This suggests that life situations are the starting points for learning rather than subject areas or information removed from the act of teaching. He feels that analysis of experience should be the prominent methodology of adult education. And since individual differences increase with age, the potential benefits from dialogue and sharing multiple perspectives are also increased.

Hunt suggests that professional development experiences should fit the conceptual levels of teachers. When we as teachers direct our inquiry, we do so on a conceptual level. Consistent with Knowles and Hunt, Sprinthall & Sprinthall suggest that teachers engage in guided reflection about experiences. They emphasise the need for us to look at teaching from a variety of perspectives and to ask ourselves, 'What does this mean to me?' and 'What does this mean to others?'. Concomitantly, they propose that there be an interactive balance between experience, discussion, and reflection. Further, they stress the need for continuous reflective activity with peer support and an awareness of our own developmental changes as they occur.

Journal writing and collegial discussion over time are consistent with, and perhaps extend, the possible developmental consequences suggested by these researchers.

Journal keeping for professional development

> . . . my most fundamental objective is to urge a change in the perception and evaluation of familiar data.
>
> THOMAS S. KUHN *The Structure of Scientific Revolutions*, pp. viii–ix.

'But how can I write about teaching? Teaching is like breathing—you just do it!', said Jerry.

'Try writing about the few events or experiences, feelings, or thoughts that occur to you as you reflect on the day', I suggested. After a few months of writing, he felt a little differently about writing and about teaching.

'I can't believe I never thought about some of these things before!' Jerry was documenting and thinking about the meaning of teaching and concomitantly exploring his own professional development.

Perceptual and phenomenological perspectives

According to Shutz (1967), 'the meaning of our experiences . . . constitutes reality' (cited in Greene 1978, p. 16). Other researchers from a perceptual, or phenomenological orientation agree. 'What is real?', asks Earl Kelley (1947). The answer is 'It all depends on your perspective'. And *that* depends on your perceptions! Perceptions are interpretations of data generated through the senses. They are dependent on (1) biological functioning, (2) experience, and (3) motivation. From a perceptual view of the individual, 'all behavior, without exception, is completely determined by, and pertinent to, the perceptual field of the behaving organism' (Combs & Snygg 1959, p. 20). We act on our perceptions. Our actions depend on (1) how we view ourselves, (2) how we view the situation, and (3) the inter-relations of our view of ourselves and the situation (Combs et al. 1971).

> The perceptual field is the universe of naive experience in which each individual lives, the everyday situation of the self and its surroundings which each person takes to be reality. To each of us the perceptual field of another contains much error and illusion; it seems an interpretation of reality rather than reality itself.
>
> (Combs & Snygg 1959, p. 21)

As teachers, then, we react to classroom events as we view them: we react to situational perceptions. When we step back from our actions, we can view them differently because we are no longer responding to a situation from the middle of it. We move beyond the immediacy of the circumstances; our perceptual fields change.

Unfortunately, once we move beyond perplexing events, we often dismiss them until they recur (sometimes in a slightly different form), and as they often relate to the same underlying problem, we are likely to continue to cope with our circumstances on an *ad hoc* basis. This sometimes 'solves' the immediate problems; sometimes it does not. If we could freeze our perceptions *at the time of our action*, we might be able to identify and understand better the underlying problems and contributing factors that are ordinarily only vaguely 'felt'. And, we could prevent many problems from recurring—we could learn from our experience.

Keeping a personal–professional journal allows us to do just that—to take snapshots of our lives as teachers. Though any snapshot enables us to view our teaching in different ways, thus contributing to improvement, it is by keeping pictures over time that we can see flows, patterns, and changes, and can thus connect events. According to Progoff (1975), writing over time allows us to establish a strong sense of our history and to position ourselves in current aspects of our development.

Integrating theory and practice

> Doubt is not a pleasant mental state but certainty is a ridiculous one.
>
> VOLTAIRE

Ignorance might be bliss, but it contributes little to professional development. In asking 'Why did I do that?', Craig found this to be the hardest question teachers can ask themselves. He found that writing and subsequent collegial discussion enabled him to explore that very question. Asking ourselves *what we do* as teachers, and *why*, is uncomfortable, but as we begin to define and to accept our behaviour and motives, we begin to define new challenges. We become increasingly aware of the complexity of teaching, and gain confidence as we view our practice.

When we write about our activity and when we return to it later, we lend two additional perspectives to it. We begin to differentiate those situations where our actions are consistent with our aims from those where they might inadvertently be working against them. For example, we sometimes get caught in the motion of events and teaching specific skills, and neglect to think about larger and long-term aims. Learning phonics, for example, should promote skill in reading, but not at the expense of an interest in, and enthusiasm for, reading.

The more we learn about our teaching, the more comfortable we become with uncertainty. Also, the more we document our teaching, the more visible is our progress.

Evaluation as a means to professional development

'How do I evaluate what I do?' 'Who sees me teach?' Few teachers view other teachers teaching (Holly 1977; Nias 1983). And, few teachers are observed after their first few years of teaching (Holly & Holly 1983), and even then observations are infrequent and for limited amounts of time. Several years ago, I asked over 100 teachers, 'If you wanted help in evaluating your work, just for your own professional development, to whom might you go?'. It came as a surprise to learn that not one teacher seemed even slightly wary of this prospect. Forty-three teachers said 'Other teachers'. The next most frequently mentioned response was 'Students' (15%), which was followed by 'Myself' (14%). When asked why they offered these responses, most teachers gave reasons like: 'It would have to be somebody who is there long enough to actually see what I do', 'It would have to be someone who would be able to tell me about teaching in a humanistic way'. Ten teachers said they would go to the principal (Holly 1977).

Too frequently, classroom observations have been conducted by evaluators who 'rated' the teacher's competence. Reports have been based on observations of teaching, and have incorporated biases and distortions based on this person's perceptions. The observer, then, to be a significant contributor to another person's professional development must be, as Jersild noted, endeavouring to identify and understand

> his own unrecognized needs, fears, desires, anxieties, hostile impulses . . . The process of gaining knowledge of self . . . is not something an instructor *teaches* others. It is not something he does *to* or *for* them. It is something in which he himself must be involved.
>
> (Jersild 1955, p. 14)

Keeping a journal and discussing what is salient to the teacher's work, with a view to improving teaching, shifts the responsibility and control of these efforts to the person who *can* make the most difference—the teacher. For teachers, writing can be an aid to clarification of assumptions and behaviour and to promoting consistency in the translation of the teacher's implicit and explicit theories into action. Professional development can branch into staff development and educational improvement.

Educational improvement: becoming a connoisseur and critic

Eisner (1979) recommends that teachers must become critics of their practice—that is, they must make public what is occurring in teaching, and what needs to happen. To be an educational critic, one must first become a connoisseur, an appreciator of significant aspects of teaching and learning. The question is 'How do teachers become connoisseurs?'. Then, 'How do teachers become critics, able and committed to share their professional concerns in public forums?'. In the portraits that follow, we will look at three teachers working on these processes. They are engaging in writing and collegial discussion as tools to analyse their teaching and learning, and to document professional development.

Teacher case studies

Judy

Writing is a chance to know myself

At 31, Judy was in her tenth year of teaching at the primary level in a medium-sized suburban community. She and her husband, Kurt, were the parents of a two-year-old daughter. Kurt, a manager in business, had a difficult time understanding why Judy spent so much of her time on school work, grading, thinking, planning, and constructing teaching aids. And, he wasn't much interested in discussing her teaching day with her.

Though the principal of Judy's school was an affable sort of fellow, and though Judy described herself as 'outgoing', she lamented the little opportunity she had to engage in meaningful professional development activity at school. 'Why isn't our inservice relevant?' 'Why can't our lounge talk be deeper? More collegial?' 'Why aren't we teachers supported professionally, commensurate with our responsibilities?'

Judy jumped at the opportunity to become part of a research project where six other teachers and the researcher were to explore teaching and professional development over a year. She, along with the other project participants, would keep a personal–professional diary and discuss her thoughts, feelings, and experiences as a teacher at weekly seminar sessions. Judy looked forward to the chance to meet other teachers and to participate in the seminar, but she began the writing with trepidation.

'What do I write about?' 'When do I write?' Because Judy was writing to explore her own teaching and professional development, she wrote as if she were talking to herself. Unlike many teachers starting from such a broad purpose, Judy immediately began to question herself on paper. She wrote of her apprehensions of working with other teachers ('I hope I'm up to working with such talented professionals!') and of dilemmas she recognised in her teaching ('Why did I do that instead of this?'). Throughout her diary are comments about her difficulty with the process of writing and especially in forming a 'writing habit', of finding time and a quiet place to reflect. She usually wrote at home at night, but sometimes during her discretionary time (art, music, lunch, recess) at school.

Judy found writing to be cathartic ('Just writing makes me feel better!'). She found that she could think on paper and work out some of her problems and dilemmas. Because she often wrote as she thought, her writing has an action quality and it isn't always in full sentences. The more she wrote, the more she was able to see patterns in her behaviour and intentions, and in her children's behaviour. She found herself writing on different levels: a surface, descriptive level and a deeper, more introspective level. She became able to differentiate which level she was writing on. She found she was able to move to the deeper level more quickly the more she wrote. She also experienced significant discomfort when she 'went in too deeply', and intentionally returned to a 'surface level' until she was ready to return to 'deeper' concerns or introspection.

Writing for Judy often became 'a contract with myself'. When she discovered something through her writing, she felt compelled to do something about it, to act on what she found out rather than to 'push it aside like I would have done before'.

What else did Judy find out about herself as a teacher? What were some of the actions she was moved to make? She was able to view herself as a finite being; she saw the humanness of her endeavours as a teacher, the complexity of her responsibilities, and she increased her ability to accept herself, to face and learn from her 'mistakes'. She saw how her feelings about (and affection toward) children influenced her teaching decisions: for example, a child was not retained whom she later found should have been ('If only I had written about David too.'). She began to see how some children received less attention than others. As she wrote about some of her frustrations, she began to identify areas of concern that she then addressed with colleagues. She found the strength and self-confidence to start raising questions and disagreeing with her administrator where previously she felt anxiety and a reticence to broach her concerns with him. On the home front (but certainly related to school), she became aware of her defensiveness and anger at her husband for his lack of interest in her teaching.

Summing up some of her thoughts on reflective writing, Judy wrote:

> **Writing**. A chance to know myself. Yes. I know myself, after all I live with myself, but this was a chance to sit down and actually confront myself. Good and bad. Self help: I made promises in . . . writing that I had to keep—levels of writing became a *way* of *thinking*. I've begun to think in terms of how I'd write about this . . . An author—for no one else but myself . . . I never knew that I could produce so much if only for me. Analysing [writing] helped me to see solutions to problems—David [for example].
>
> As I look back, I realise that I needed to be more objective . . . I couldn't see some existing problems . . . I was really close to my class. Because of writing, I'm beginning to see that again . . .
>
> As I look at children, I try to really 'see' them, their daily lives, what affects them. I also see things more indepth; I analyse more. This is a major result of my writing. It's helped me to do this . . . I'm a better teacher . . . I feel more confident . . . I'm able to handle stress better . . .

Carole

> The writing itself was very beneficial to me personally because it made me look at my teaching philosophy and how I was dealing with students, parents, and administrators. I was forced through writing to take a look at myself.

Carole was born in a large northern city in the Midwest in the winter of 1951. The middle child of a large family, she took responsibility (like her older sisters) for her younger siblings while their mother worked as a domestic to support the family. 'Carole will be the teacher in this family', her mother frequently reminded them. Like many of her friends, Carole was assisted in her education by the Follow-Through Program (a federally funded US program set up to alleviate inequality between social groups in schools) for promising children from low-income families. Her studies were difficult at the small nearby liberal arts college she attended, but with hard work and help in developing study skills from Follow-Through, she graduated and became 'the teacher in this family'.

Having taught at the primary level in two inner-city schools in her home town, Carole and her new husband, John, moved to a small college town about an hour's drive away. Carole began teaching in a system that was culturally different from her. As the only Black teacher, she often felt lonely, though people were 'friendly'.

During her ninth year of teaching, she, along with Judy and five other teachers, joined a project to look at teaching and professional development. Very active in the local and state teachers' organisation and in the minority caucus (an organisation to further racial, ethnic, and cultural understanding), Carole brought unique perspectives to the exploration of teaching and professional development. At the same time, she separated from her husband.

Carole began writing by jotting down topics as they occurred to her and expanding on them later. Her style of writing was fairly formal. She wrote in complete thoughts and sentences, and rarely, if ever, rewrote or extended her thoughts in the margins. The act of writing was not difficult, but finding time to tuck away, given full teaching and professional organisation commitments, church, and an exercise schedule wasn't easy. She, like Judy, found writing to be cathartic.

She found herself unleashing on paper 'many of the frustrations that had accumulated during my first eight years of teaching'. She was surprised by her complaints, not realising, she said, that she kept them inside.

> When I first began writing, I cited mainly those things about teaching that were not to my satisfaction. When I look back . . . I was very disenchanted about where I was as a teacher and my enthusiasm as a teacher. I had thought many times about leaving this profession . . . just to get a break from the many demands that teachers receive from students, administrators, parents and the community.

Recording her frustrations and sharing some of them with colleagues seemed to allow Carole to focus more on her teaching. She wrote of dilemmas, and began to use her diary to record research as she undertook to learn more from the children. For one thing, she focused on reading and language arts. This had been a source of frustration for her, for, she discovered, several reasons. A reading consultant spent a day or two a week in the building, but worked with very few of Carole's children. Yet to Carole's disgruntlement, the consultant made decisions on what individual children 'should be reading'. But how does she know? She doesn't even *know* these children!', Carole moaned. A new reading series had been adopted and Carole and her colleagues had their hands full mastering the more complex and comprehensive program. Not long before report-card time, reading tests were administered, followed by orders from the reading consultant that children were to be graded, based on standardised scores on the test. 'But I could have moved the children along faster had I known before it would determine their grades', lamented Carole.

Carole wrote of her frustrations, of her growing understanding of the series, and of her research with the children regarding reading and language arts. 'What is reading to the children?', she wondered. So, she conducted a survey. From this and subsequent study, she learned more about how the children thought and felt about aspects of the curriculum. She began to recognise the differences in perception between herself and the children, and among individual children.

Another area Carole selected to study was maths. She found that 'lots of times they are able to do the work correctly but very seldom do they truly understand the process they are using'. She was surprised at the children's candour and honesty in offering their opinions when she questioned them. At the end of the year 'they remembered vividly the times we had popcorn in maths class and the time we used lollipops for counting ... for next school year I should work on making maths more fun for *all* students'. (Children were grouped for maths and not every group experienced the lessons the children found most enjoyable and that Carole found to be most productive.)

In addition to finding out more about how her children experienced school and increasing her knowledge about their home lives, Carole learned some significant things about herself:

> I began to appreciate myself and my contribution to education. I began to realise that it's not what others think of me as a teacher but how I view myself. Several times I wrote about the need for praise from administrators and I'm sure that this is a need that I have and many other teachers also share.

Carole found the 'praise' she sought in her writing and she began to appreciate the subtle (and sometimes not so subtle!) indications of growth and satisfaction from the children.

Carole feels that she is more aware and more sensitive to the needs of children and to the complexity of teaching. She learned that 'I have faults that I was not aware of ... my attachment to my students affects my life outside of school and perhaps my relationship with my spouse'. She learned that 'there are certain things that I'll never be able to change'. And, through collegial discussion, she learned that 'the same problems I've had difficulty dealing with are common to other teachers too'.

Perhaps of greatest significance to Carole, she began to see the interactive nature of her home and school lives. According to Carole, the most influential factor in her school life was her personal problems at home: 'Because things were lacking in my marriage, I devoted much time to my teaching and became very attached to my students'. Having discovered the consuming role that teaching played in her life, Carole resolved to work towards a better balance.

Jerry

How often do we question ourselves?

The thought of becoming a teacher didn't occur to Jerry until he was 22 and had been in the Air Force for four years. In fact, the idea of college had until then been 'something for other people'. It was there he met Sue, who later became his wife. Sue is a school psychologist and, according to Jerry, 'It's great to have a spouse in a related field. She understands my job and I hers'.

Jerry has spent six years teaching in the primary grades at a kindergarten-through-grade-two school in an upper-middle-class bedroom community (14 000 population) bordering a middle-sized industrial city. The school system has a fine reputation and Jerry feels quite comfortable working with the children.

Writing was not new to Jerry. He wrote poetry and occasionally kept diary-like notes on topics of interest to him, 'just for me though, I enjoy writing'. Writing about his own teaching and professional development was new. 'But how can I write about teaching? Teaching is like breathing—you just do it!' Jerry began by writing about individual children. He wrote journalistically, descriptively, and subjectively. He later commented on his previous writing, 'My biases shine!'. He wrote of his teaching day, of incidents that amused or perplexed him. He also wrote about his conversations with his closest colleagues, Beverly, Jane, and Karen.

Writing, like his composing of poetry, working construction, and playing the guitar and singing, is a form of creative expression for Jerry. Writing is cathartic, and for the most part he enjoys the process more than the product.

He found himself taking side journeys into language, and would think on words and phrases and their meanings and values. 'What is "good"?', he mused and proceeded to define the different uses of the word 'good'. Jerry found that the longer he wrote, the more aware he became of his teaching and of happenings around the school and of his interactions with others. Jerry felt that this increasing attention to detail and attending to events as they happened was largely due to his growing habit of looking at his teaching life 'as if I was going to write about it even when I'm not planning to'. While Jerry saw many benefits of this growing awareness, it posed some real difficulties too.

'This self-inspection' Jerry found himself engaged in was often quite disconcerting. He felt the urge to return to more carefree times and places, and during one particularly difficult (and growth-producing) time, he said,

> I've come back away from looking at myself because I think I went too far
> . . . I think in writing . . . we are questioning ourselves . . . and I think there
> is very little precedent set for us to do that. Yet, I think when we look at
> the whole concept of professional growth, that's a piece of it. Yes, you have
> to do it.

Jerry moved from purely descriptive writing to exploratory and introspective writing. His writing became less a story that he was telling and more of an inquiry:

> As I review my writings and inspect myself I see more and more the need
> for patience. Furthermore, I am seeing patience as a practised art . . . How
> often do I respond in the classroom when I should be biting my tongue and
> practising patience? I have to wonder about my role [as teacher] as teller.

Commenting on his writing at the end of the project, Jerry wrote,

> the journal was a close inspection. A chance, a delightful chance for me to
> speak my subjective mind and have someone actually read it. It makes all

the difference in the world. It was often a chore. I realise, now, because I didn't necessarily want to confront myself. The journal offered insights and revealed a lot of my inner self to me. It admits that I care and commits me to my observations. Scary in a way. How often do we question ourselves?

A very important concomitant to writing, for Jerry, was collegial discussion. Though he began writing 'for himself only', he slowly began to share his ideas and selected parts of his writing with other teachers. Writing and discussion became interactively supportive of his professional development. Sometimes he stated his problems before he wrote about them; other times he wrote about them and then spoke with colleagues about them.

I'm glad to know I do not stand alone … defending one's position often calls for *reflection and close inspection*. Even while wrestling with my own feelings and motives verbally, I was always received with compassion and understanding. No better feeling than to trust one's peers enough to strip the veneer which masks your motives; inspect yourself and redress, to face tomorrow a bit more prepared.

Jerry discovered how much of his home life influenced his school life and vice versa. He discovered the significance of professional dialogue, and how important 'trust' was to enable reflection with others and with himself. 'I can say I've grown reflective. I move a bit slower—to savor instead of merely taste. I enjoy. I yield. I trust myself more—it opens many doors.'

Part 3: The journal — a writer's manual

Introduction

As you approach the task of actually writing your journal, it is important to keep in mind the *personal* aspect of the personal–professional journal — to clarify the relationship of your journal to *you*.

Writing for yourself

First and foremost, you are writing for yourself. Journal writing, as it has been described here, is a process of reflection to enable you to become more aware of your teaching and professional development as you are experiencing and directing them. What you write, when you write, how you write, and what you share with others are up to you. You will probably, like others, find that writing for yourself is therapeutic, that you can write to describe events, thoughts, and feelings that were previously taken for granted or easily forgotten. You will find that writing is a useful tool for capturing ideas to consider that will enable you to clarify your thinking, pose new questions, and pursue issues only dimly perceived before. You may want to focus on individual children and the circumstances of your teaching. You will probably find yourself writing about problems, and through the writing process, identifying possible solutions. At the same time, you may find the burden or image of the problem reduced to a more manageable size. For example, as Craig reread his journal, he was surprised by the emotion and feelings that he found in his writing. As he relived the experiences about which he had written, he was able to understand why seemingly trivial events often loomed large in his teaching day. Now, when he begins to feel 'pressed', he steps out and re-evaluates the situation: 'I can now recognise problems before they turn into big ones. I can stop molehills from becoming mountains. Then I have the energy to see the *real* mountains'.

Writing to communicate

Another important dimension of journal writing is the sharing of ideas with a colleague (or colleagues). As you focus on your teaching, and your concerns become more visible to you, you will be better able to discuss them with others. Often in teaching, we feel a nagging anxiety, even irritation, that we are unable to define. Writing about how we feel and the circumstances leading to these feelings, and surrounding them, enables us to understand them better, to bring them from abstract feelings to concrete problems. Writing for ourselves and defining factors leading to anxiety helps to make discussion possible. Each restatement, whether writing, reflecting, or discussing, brings us to a slightly different perspective.

Writing to communicate with others can stem from, or be an expansion of, journal writing. This can take many different forms. Kate, another primary teacher, for example, found herself planning on paper, and deciding to share a segment of her journal with her principal. He added a few comments and questions; they discussed her ideas; and she now frequently plans on paper and sends him copies rather than the more specific short-term lesson plans she previously turned in to the office each week. David, a high-school English teacher, finds that when he wants to talk with a colleague or administrator about a specific concern, he benefits from first sending the person a brief note explaining the main topics he wishes to discuss. According to David, this begins their discussion on a common note. He finds it is often difficult to communicate his concerns orally and then take the discussion to a fruitful conclusion. Given constraints on time for collegial discussion, he finds that the discussion wanders and people interpret his concerns from their own viewpoints. When he takes the time to write his ideas, he feels there is much less chance for misunderstanding:

> It is easier for people to bring their own agendas, to hear what they *think* you are saying rather than what you are *actually* saying when conversation is out of the blue. When you convey your concerns in writing this is much less likely to occur. Then they have time to think about it and come back to it.

I have found in my experience that after I have written ideas for communication to others, I am more able to speak clearly (and concisely) to the topic.

A third audience for writing might consist of parents, the community, and others. Eisner (1979) eloquently calls our attention to the need for teachers to be connoisseurs and critics of teaching and education. To be a critic, one must first be a connoisseur—that is, an appreciator of significant aspects and elements of teaching and society; then one must be able to convey these to others, to make public important dimensions that only a connoisseur, one close to the process of education, can make clear. This is probably more necessary now than it has been in the past. Teachers and schooling have been held up to public scrutiny, criticised, if not pointedly, then by implication, in public analysis of test scores and the consequent call for accountability. Teachers have been singled out as 'low scorers' on college aptitude/achievement tests (Vance & Schlechty 1982) and for the first time in the United States, education and the quality of schools and teachers are a major political issue. As teachers, we now have people's attention. It is up to us to study and to articulate to parents and others what we know about teaching and learning.

Beginning

Choosing materials

The first thing you will need to do is to select materials for your writing. To some people, this is not a particularly important consideration. They write on school notebooks, scrap paper, mimeograph paper, or whatever paper is available at the time they wish to write. For others of us, it is important to select specific materials that will make it more comfortable to write over a period of time. Simons (1978) suggests that durability, size, and flexibility be considered.

Durability. Is it important that it be durable? Will you want to carry your journal with you? Or will it be stationary—will you leave it on your desk at home or at school?

Size. Where you intend to write will make a difference in the size journal you select. If you intend to carry it with you, you will need to find a size that is both durable and small enough to transport comfortably. Smaller journals, though easier to carry, are more difficult to write in. Stenographer pads have the benefit of wire loops, which make it easier to open them flat for writing. Large notebooks or journal pads are easier to write in, but they are more difficult to carry.

Flexibility. Both small and large books for journal keeping are available in stationery shops and book shops. They sometimes contain fairly high-quality paper and have attractive and durable covers like other hard-cover books. Like books, they are bound. They have the added advantage of keeping all of your writing together in one place, and, because of their 'permanent' and 'professional' format, they dissuade the writer from tearing out pages (which at the moment seem better thrown out, but later might be very important to understanding; just as we might not like to remember yesterday's cold rain, we are thankful for it when the flowers bloom). Loose-leaf notebooks, on the other hand, do not appear quite so professional, nor is the quality of paper as good. They have the advantage of flexibility, though. Pages can be removed (don't throw them away!) and sections reorganised as ideas develop through your experience in journal keeping. Many of us find it useful to carry on a dialogue between different parts of our journal. Progoff (1975), for example, suggests that it is important to keep several sections and to allow momentum and energy to develop as a result of interactive dialogue among the different sections. His sections include a history, a daily log, and several others. If it is, or becomes, important to you to divide your journal into sections, you might wish to select a journal format that permits you this flexibility.

I find it most convenient to keep a regular-sized, loose-leaf notebook and to either write on standard, lined paper or punch holes in unlined paper. This way I can write on any paper and insert it. I find that this gives me the opportunity to write wherever and whenever I choose and to insert it in the journal when I can. I also find it important to select a pen or pencil that fits my mood. Usually that is a fine-point black pen that allows me freedom to write quickly and easily. Sometimes I want to write with a broader, subtler edge and the feeling of resistance that a pencil permits. Occasionally I write with more than one colour. At times, red 'feels' right; at other times, it's green. Allow yourself to develop your writing according to your senses. You might even develop your own colour-coding system. For example, as you reread some of your entries, you might wish to add comments in the margins or in the body of the text in another colour. This promotes an understanding of the multiple perspectives you will develop as you look at your writing at different times.

Some of us find it useful to use unlined paper when we wish to sketch or include other materials such as journal and newspaper excerpts or our children's work. A loose-leaf notebook permits these different kinds of entries.

Choosing a focus

You might wish to start your journal with a short autobiography. This will help you to locate yourself in the context of growth—to get a sense of where you have come from. In order to do that, you might ask yourself these sorts of questions:

- Why did you become a teacher?
- When and how did you decide?
- What and who influenced you?
- In what ways?
- As you look back, possibly to your first years of schooling, what feelings and images remain?
- Which teachers do you remember, and why do you remember them?
- What do you remember about them?
- Focus on one or two teachers who you really felt helped you.
- Why do you think they were helpful?
- What were the most meaningful aspects of your education (including teacher education) that contributed to your development as a teacher?
- If you could make the decision again to become a teacher, would you?
- Why, or why not?
- What do you see as your greatest strengths as a teacher?
- What would you like to change or work on to improve your teaching?
- What are a few of the frustrations you face as a teacher?
- The joys and satisfactions?
- What are a few of the hopes you have for the children you teach?

You might write some of these questions to begin your journal, and leave others for later entries. How you proceed to use your journal will depend on your reasons for writing. Some teachers have found it useful to begin by sitting down at the end of the day and recalling incidents that stand out: thoughts, feelings, and meaningful events with children, anything about which they wish to write. You might begin your writing by jotting down topics as they occur to you during the day. Some people find it useful to write for brief periods throughout the day or week, as the opportunities arise.

It is often helpful to record your thoughts and feelings about writing and the journal-keeping process. As one teacher noted, 'It helps to get me started', and another, 'Just writing down my apprehensions about writing lessens them'.

It might be easier to write about some of your experiences and plans if you talk them out first, either with yourself or, if possible, with a colleague. Some people find it helpful to talk into a tape-recorder—by themselves or with a colleague. They play the tape back and stop it at times to write.

If you are writing as a tool for documentation, and in a systematic way to focus on specific aspects of your teaching, you might begin by writing about the process of professional development on which you would like to concentrate. You might, for example, be preparing to engage in curriculum development, staff development with colleagues, professional development such as clinical supervision (focusing on specific teaching behaviour in collaboration with a colleague), or action research (focusing on a problem or question; planning action; implementing change; documenting, and reflecting on, what happened). Using journal writing for description, documentation, and analysis can be even more helpful if you include your comments on the processes of action and change *as they occur*. This includes your reservations, hopes, and challenges as you engage with others in the process.

Choosing a time and place

You might find that after you write for a few weeks, you will begin to 'see' and to be more aware of your professional and teaching life as it evolves, almost as if you are mentally taking details to write about.

There are basically three time periods to consider for writing in your journal. For some experiences, you will probably wish to write about plans and ideas *before something occurs*. Perhaps you want to try out a new lesson, organise the day in a new way, or have a colleague observe an aspect of your teaching or a given activity in your room. Use your journal to think through what, and how, and why you are going to do something. What are some possible consequences? Planned? Incidental?

Another time to record is *as close to the time of the experience* as possible. Usually this will consist of a few key words and phrases that will be of help to you in reconstructing the events later. When you write at the time of the occurrence (or soon after), it is often worthwhile to jot down images and feelings. These make reflection easier later. The third time for writing is *after the experience* occurs, and according to Progoff (1975), the sooner after, the better. We tend to remember experiences selectively, and the closer in time to the occurrence, the less likely we are to omit or change important details to fit how we might want to remember them. In other instances, the distance of time will be beneficial.

Many people find a quiet time at night to think back over events they then record in their journals. Some teachers sit down at school, after the children leave, to quietly record in their journals events that took place in school. They find it easier to visualise what happened in the classroom by writing there. Other teachers write journal entries in snatches when time is available throughout the week. One time to record, they find, is when they are making out lesson plans. A few teachers I have worked with set aside time within the school day for journal writing—their own and their children's. Marcia, a Year 4 teacher, finds this a good way to start the day. She leaves her journal open on her desk so the children may read it if they wish. Both Marcia and the children may read it if they wish. Both Marcia and the children select writing to share and keep personal writing private.

Whenever you choose to write, it is important that you leave enough time to reflect quietly—this means time away from other demands. Though this is often a difficult habit to form, especially when we are so used to 'hurrying' and 'action', it quickly becomes a looked-forward-to time, and we wonder why we haven't protected some 'thought time' for ourselves before!

For many of us, the place we choose to write is as important as the time. For example, while jotting down descriptive comments, ideas, and impressions (to expand on later) might conveniently take place in the teacher's lounge, this is rarely a place where quiet, reflective writing can take place. According to Progoff (1975), we need a quiet place where we can contemplate by ourselves, and a comfortable chair or sofa where we can let the tensions of the day slowly recede. Where you write depends on the type of writing you are going to do. Craig leaves his journal on his desk and writes throughout the week, as close to occurrences as he can. Then, on Sunday evenings, he sets aside time to reflect and write. Judy writes a few days a week either before or after school for a short time and then relaxes when the week is over on Friday evenings with a pencil and paper to write (sometimes describing events, other times working out concerns, sometimes introspectively). You might find that for descriptive writing, a quiet place and time is not necessary, while for reflective, introspective writing, it is.

Most of us find it important, especially before a writing habit is formed, to plan time for writing into our schedules. Though writing seems at first a time-consuming endeavour, most of us find that we are 'saving' time by becoming aware of where we are efficient in our use of time and where we are not.

What to write about?

The possible topics and experiences you might record in your journal are limited only by your imagination. You might document your thoughts, feelings, questions, statements, plans, descriptions, analyses, and introspection as you explore teaching and professional development. This means that you might focus some of your writing on each of three dimensions of your professional life: (1) teaching—what you do and why; (2) students—what they do, the circumstances, a description of their behaviour, thoughts, and feelings; and (3) collegial interactions and the process of professional development—your thoughts and feelings as you approach writing and collegial discussion, as you plan, reflect on, and engage in exploration of teaching and professional development.

Teaching roles and responsibilities. What do you do and why do you do it? What circumstances surrounded your behaviour? What led to the actions you took? What do you think and feel about what you did? What might you do if a similar circumstance exists in the future? Do you see any patterns emerging in your behaviour. What aspects of your teaching do you want to focus on?

Students. What do students (or does a student) do? What behaviour is unusual? What behaviour is consistent over time? What students are you particularly concerned about? Might short descriptive comments entered over time enable you to better understand the student? Might it be helpful to concentrate on your work with a student or group over time, documenting and discussing progress?

Collegial interaction and professional development. How do you feel about writing? What thoughts crop up when you think about writing? When you write? How do you feel about sharing your writing, your thoughts and feelings, about your teaching and professional development with a colleague? Colleagues? Who might be able to lend their support and a different perspective? How might they be helpful to you? You to them?

Over time you will begin to connect writing in different dimensions of your teaching life as relationships begin to emerge. What you write about is important, but of even greater importance is your relationship to what you write. The extent to which you are able to describe your behaviour and your relationship to the circumstances and actions you describe in your journal will in part determine what you can learn from them. Writing, as we have seen, can be a cathartic process. It can also promote change. Though writing down your impressions, your joys, and your frustrations is valuable in itself, there might be little change in practice unless the process is taken further. As Jackson (1971) pointed out, in order to benefit from experience, we must reflect on it, cogitate over it, and try to make sense of it, from a distance. Recording our thoughts and feelings in a journal enables us to return to them from a different perspective.

How to develop your writing style

Everyone has a personal style of writing. Because few of us are professional writers and therefore spend little time writing to convey our thoughts to others, we usually do not give much thought to the process of writing. We are probably unaware of our writing style. As we write more and think more about what we are writing and how best to convey ideas, we will begin to define our style.

Most of us learned specific rules of grammar, which we try to employ as we write. When we read over our writing, it often sounds stilted or formal. We think that writing is like talking, but what we have written does not sound like our speech. If we become overly concerned with how we write, we may abandon writing—or at least turn it into a mechanical procedure. This is not to say that there are not grammatical rules and conventions involved in writing. As a general rule, concentrate first on conveying ideas vividly, using sensory experiences, and then concentrate on clarity and succinctness. Approached in this way, rules of grammar can help us to communicate more clearly. Style is rarely a conscious development; it develops as we write and rewrite.

Two final suggestions might be useful.

Relax. Though you will not always be relaxed when you write, it is important that you are often. You will find yourself writing quickly and allowing your senses to push out the words more quickly than you 'think' of them. This is how it should be. It is important to allow yourself to relax and to let the motion of the day subside—to let an inner peace take over. For this, you might protect a time and a place that are yours—where you can feel yourself unwind. Like practising yoga, this is the time to 'reconcile the peace of asana with the press of life' (Burke 1983, p. 40). Just a few minutes of quiet time, when you allow your breathing to become deeper and slower, can set the tone for reflective writing. For Judy, this means sitting down on Friday night with a glass of wine and relaxing with her journal after a physically, emotionally, socially, and intellectually demanding week of teaching. Others of us find it both releasing and renewing to weave ourselves into music, to lift ourselves from both the past and the future into a present that experiences only itself. Regardless of how you remove yourself from outward action, the important point is that you do so.

Write vividly. When you are recording your experiences, try to describe them as vividly as you can. Try to transport the reader (you will be the reader) to your experience. This means: include as much detail as you need to convey the images, thoughts, feelings, and occurrences as they happened. As you gain practice in writing, you will probably enjoy the challenges of translating your experiences into words and of recapturing a sense of the circumstances. When you take a snapshot, for example, you try to frame it as artistically as you can. You want to capture what you see. When you view the picture, it enables you to return to the circumstances, to remember what you said and felt. There is a caveat though. What you see in a snapshot is only a likeness of reality—it is not reality. Reality moves. It is in a constant state of change, and it can be viewed in multiple dimensions. When you write, it is well to keep in mind the transitory and 'unreal' nature of your reconstructions. Your words are a partial picture derived from experience at a specific time—a segment of a flowing process:

> Thoughts, ideas, and words are 'coins' for real things. They are *not* those things, and though they represent them, there are many ways in which they do not correspond at all . . . ideas and words are more or less fixed, whereas real things change.
>
> (Watts 1951, p. 45)

According to Watts (1951), 'the power of words must have seemed magical [when they were first used], and, indeed, the miracles which verbal thinking has wrought have justified the impression' (pp. 45-6). But, he cautions, 'to define has come to mean almost the same thing as to under stand' (p. 46).

Keeping in mind that we are never able to return to our experiences, which are real only when occurring, it will be helpful to describe them as vividly as we can so that the images we retain will be as close as possible to meaningful dimensions of the experiences.

D

Writing reflectively about practice

> . . . travelling outward and inward at the same time is less a matter of physical impossibility than a condition of mental health and moral well being.
>
> T. MALLON, *A Book of One's Own*

There are two major dimensions of practice to explore: the personal and the professional-collegial. Through journal writing we see how these are interrelated and integrated. We see, as Erikson (1975) noted, 'psychosocial' beings. We are unique beings who live and work in social worlds and historical periods. In the last chapter we addressed topics to write about (teaching, students, professional and collegial activity) which provide broad general guidelines for writing. In this chapter, more specific suggestions for exporing practice are presented. In the first section we will address ways to probe the personal dimension of practice and in the second we will look at ways to investigate the professional-collegial.

Finally, because few of us have written journals about our teaching before, there are bound to be some questions that will arise. Many of these have been addressed in previous sections of this book. I will summarise some of the more common concerns here under the headings of:

- the writing process,
- forming the writing habit,
- writing as a tool for analysis,
- writing to promote self-understanding, and
- collegial discussion.

Exploring the Personal Dimension of the Professional

Since we bring our histories with us when we enter the classroom, it is important to reflect on the ways our past experiences influence our thoughts, feelings, and behaviour as teachers. As adults, we are able to 'look at our own looking' and analyse our experiences. Children, and most adolescents, are not developmentally ready to do this. They do not usually question their own behaviour; they do not ask themselves 'Now why did I do that?' As professionals, we must ask ourselves that question, and, we must consider our answers. This entails making explicit many of the tacit assumptions, beliefs, and rationales that guide our teaching. You might wish to devote a section of your journal to autobiographical and 'life historical' writing. The following journal exercises are designed to help us to become aware of experiences in our pasts that help to define us as teachers.

Life History Timeline. Divide your life into sections on a timeline. Use divisions such as: early childhood, early elementary school years, later elementary years, junior high or middle school years, high school years, college years, and adulthood. Below each section write key words or phrases to describe what comes to mind as you reflect on this time. After you have gone through the entire timeline and noted some of your experiences, see if you can characterise this period with a brief description of the most important aspects of the time (geographical move, birth, illness, new school). The purpose is to briefly, but comprehensively, sketch your life. As a follow-up on separate paper write about each period in greater detail, recalling events and people as vividly as you can. Consult old photo albums, slides, and any other artifacts you might have.

Above the timeline, write your recollection of what was happening in the society (and world perhaps) in which you were living. What were the most significant events? What people were most influential? What major legislation passed during these years? This can be a real adventure if you decide to use the library for research into major events. Civil rights legislation in the United States of America, in the 1960s, for example, ushered in significant changes in the lives of most of us.

As you look at your timeline, what do you notice? What thoughts occur to you about your life? What relationships do you find among and between the three parts of this chart (the line and your age, below the line and your experiences, and above the line and the societal conditions and events)?

Vignettes of Life, People, and Schooling. A vignette is a little story, a brief account, or a picture of an experience. Select an event from the past (or a person) and describe it as vividly as you can. Take yourself back to an early schooling experience. Describe it in detail. Reconstruct the scene as if you were there or as if it had happened yesterday. Who was there? What happened and what did you think and feel?

Portraits of People and Experience. A portrait is a picture of a person, place, or event. It is a rendering of what the writer perceives to be of most value. It can be composed from vignettes, or a vignette can begin or end the portrait. Write a portrait of a person from your past. What are the most distinguishing characteristics of this person? Or, what one word would you use to characterise this person? Perhaps, it is a humorous experience you remember. Use this to guide your portrait construction. Write only about things that relate to this experience. Exaggerate to make your point. Now, try writing a self-portrait. Pick a time in your life to characterise in your portrait. Perhaps a delightful, or a painful experience during adolescence. Write about yourself as you might be writing about someone else, or as if you were telling a story that someone who didn't know you would read. Try to capture the 'character' you were.

One of the most beneficial aspects of portrait construction is that you learn more about others and about yourself through the process of construction. Regardless of who you write a portrait of, what you write is a reflection of you. And, when you write a self-portrait, you become the observed. As Albert Camus noted 'I am happy to be both halves, the watcher and the watched'. (Mallon 1984, p. 143)

Exploring Professional-Collegial Aspects of Teaching

Though professional development is of necessity a personal process, it is also a social and collegial one. Looking inward, becoming aware as professionals is intertwined with looking outward, learning from and contributing to, the profession. Part of our contribution is helping to shape the profession and the environment within which we work. What defines the profession of teaching? In what ways can we work with our colleagues to improve schooling? The following suggestions for journal writing are designed to help us focus on teaching and collaboration with our colleagues. **Interviewing.** One of the most useful tools for learning is asking questions. Everyday we greet colleagues with, 'Hi, how are you?' We wait for a brief reply, and continue on our way, or we stay and talk about something else. What if we asked, 'Hi. How is your day going?' or 'What is happening in your classroom today?' or 'What satisfactions do you get from being a teacher?' or 'What have been the most meaningful events in your classroom this week?' and actually stay around long enough to listen to the response. Typically, we know very little about most fellow staff members. Informal and semi-structured interviews within a school can provide valuable information for staff and program development as well as promote a professional and collegial school climate. Ask teachers to write down their thoughts on a question of common interest and ask that this be on the agenda for discussion at the next faculty meeting.

I Searches. As teachers we are inquirers and problem solvers, even, researchers. Unfortunately we are often unaware of our own questions and responses because they happen so quickly and so naturally as part of the 'implicit' responsibilities of teaching. Recording some of our inquiry makes it possible to see our progress and share our concerns and progress with others. The 'I Search' is a procedure for writing our 'searches'. It is a method used by a professor of English, Ken Macrorie, who decided that research writing was not very helpful to students trying to learn to write. Very simply, the 'I Search' is the story of trying to find something out and what you find out. It is the story of your search, not someone else's (as research so often is). Rather than going straight to the library to get information, you begin with those persons around you who might be helpful. The procedure is as follows: What do you want to find out about? Who might have this information? How might you go about it? What did you do? And, what did you find out? 'I Search' writing is journal writing that describes your problem solving.

Case Studies. A case study is a study of a person, a situation or a problem. It means focusing on something and gathering related information. It is a more formal method of recording your inquiry than an 'I Search'. The case study can be explanatory, exploratory, or descriptive. Many teachers conduct case studies of children in their classrooms. They begin to record information on the child and note behaviour related to their interest. Cindy, a kindergarten teacher, for example, was concerned about a new child in her room who could not speak English and was too shy to interact with other children. She began to write daily about the child, recording behaviour and her own efforts to help. After a month of recording her observations, Cindy had figured out several ways to help the child adjust to her new classroom and the other children. Cindy wrote a summary of the 'case' and documented what had happened to the child. She found, as she analysed and wrote the summary that she had changed as a teacher too. One of the benefits of case-study writing for teachers is that we begin to observe more sensitively and with more focus. It removes us from some of the motion of teaching long enough to devote our energies to specific problems. As in any kind of writing that involves other people, a case study should be addressed and conducted with caution, care, and professional judgment. The case-study method, as it is recommeded here, is for our own use and the privacy and protection of the persons involved must be uppermost in our deliberations. Even though the case is written in your journal, it is advisable to use a ficticious name for the child you are trying to understand. A case study, like a portrait, is often as descriptive of the author as it is of the subject.

The following methods of inquiry involve collaboration with a colleague.

Action Research. A case study can be conducted without any intention of change. It may be done for understanding alone (though this can certainly precipitate change in behaviour). Action research, in contrast, is research undertaken with the intention of improving conditions. Ebbutt defines action research as 'the systematic study of attempts to change and improve educational practice by groups of participants by means of their own practical actions and by means of their own reflection upon the effects of those actions' (1985, p. 156).

Let us say that the teachers in your school have written about their concerns, these have been discussed in a faculty meeting, and it has been agreed that the staff will focus on improving parent–teacher relationships. Action research is documenting what the staff defines as the problem, what the plans are for alleviating present difficulties, what actions are taken, and what results from these efforts. One action-research project often leads to another. For example, once you have improved parent–teacher relations, you may collaboratively decide to work on improving the school climate, or designing and implementing a parent volunteer program.

Clinical Supervision. Focusing on teaching is a difficult process. There is so much to pay attention to! And, it can be a very lonely endeavor. Somehow the successful experiences we have are too easily overshadowed by the difficulties we have. One 'bad' experience can blot out ten 'good' ones. Working with a colleague can help prevent some of the frustrations we feel and offer the support that can lead to confidence and change. The aim of clinical supervision is to help teachers to gain control over their own teaching as well as their development as professionals (Smyth 1984). It is a method for collaboratively studying (and changing) teaching.

The method involves working with a trusted colleague who agrees to help you develop your teaching (and implicitly your ability to reflect on your teaching). Ideally, the process is reciprocal; you help each other focus on practice. The steps involved are:

1   *A pre-observation conference* where you discuss what you want the person to observe in your classroom (for example, your question asking, or non-verbal language, classroom interaction patterns);

2   *The observation* in which the teacher observes a lesson noting what you agreed on as the focus for observation;

3   *The descriptive analysis of teaching* which includes the observer giving you notes from the observation; and

4   *The post-observation conference* where you both discuss what you have analysed from the notes.

Reading and then reacting to this reading in your journal is another good way to explore the profession. You can reflect on ideas and their suitability for teaching. This is one of the ways in which writers prepare themselves for writing. They record their reactions to the writing of other people and they assess it. They sometimes compare it to others' writing and to their own. Questions such as 'Which of the schools presented in *The Good High School* (Lightfoot 1984) reminds me of mine? Why? and 'How could I adapt Calkin's suggestions in *The Art of Teaching Writing* (1986) to my classroom?' provide alternative lenses for viewing teaching.

Each of these methods for studying teaching and documenting inquiry can help us to be more aware and articulate spokespersons for our profession, an important step in shaping the kinds of professional environments within which we can direct and learn from experience.

The writing process

'But what should I write about?' What you write about is much less important than the process of writing, of establishing on paper some of the things that you do as a teacher. Let your writing evolve from your interest, from meaningful aspects of your teaching, from dilemmas or challenges you might like to explore further. Select an experience and write about it soon after you experience it (unless you would like to write about something you remember from the past). Simply write as you think about it. Better yet, try to take yourself back and capture on paper how it felt at the time—write as many details as you can remember. You might find it useful to expand on your experiences later, but don't be concerned with this. You might also find it beneficial to select a few segments of your writing to extend and polish. Work on clarifying your thoughts through your writing and work to present your thoughts (and feelings) in a way that conveys the experiences at the time they occurred. Such brief, polished vignettes help us to convey the weight and colour of small aspects of our lives as teachers and to feel competent as writers. At first many of us would rather not look back at our writing. Reasons for this include: not wanting to appear incompetent; not wanting to relive our teaching;

and not wanting to look at behaviours after the event. What we see, however, is: how we grow and change; how the immediate circumstances of our teaching contextualise our behaviours; and how (with polished writing) pleasantly articulate we can become.

We aren't used to writing to ourselves. Most writing has been for our teachers and professors and it has been structured for us. In our journal writing, we are asked to identify and write about our own concerns, our own ideas and feelings. Here is a chance to be listened to—to be seriously attended to, to clarify our thoughts to share with others—and we are guaranteed an interested colleague—ourselves!

Forming the writing habit

Removing ourselves from the motion in our teaching lives long enough to write reflectively about them is no small task. Whether writing is more easily done in snatches throughout the week or in longer periods once or more a week will depend on you.

When *could* you write? Look at your potential time for professional dialogue. How important is time for reflection? Worth 30 minutes a day? Two hours a week? Four? It is important to realise that you will not always write as you have planned to. When you do not write, do not worry or feel guilty about it. Resume as soon as you can and make notes of important occurrences since you last wrote. Do not try to include too much. Instead, move on to more current experiences.

Writing as a tool for analysis

For many of us it is difficult to write descriptively without including our interpretations. Our interpretations can be very useful, but we need to recognise that they are interpretations and as such change as our perspectives change. Some teachers find it helpful to go back over their writing and to note (by underlining or bracketing) passages of interpretation. Interpretations can add much to our understanding of experiences, but it is helpful to recognise them as one perspective among several possible perspectives. Another approach that teachers have found helpful in differentiating factual information from influences is to divide journal entries into 'sides', one side for description of the facts (information that several observers might agree on) and one side for interpretations (and, possibly implications).

Another important way to learn about your teaching is to allow yourself time to sit in quiet reflection, clearing your mind and returning to images that recur from the day, or few days since you last wrote. This helps to highlight significant experiences, which might otherwise go unnoticed. It also brings us closer to our experiences before we have a chance to judge or edit them.

Regardless of the format you decide to use for your writing, you will probably find it useful to date and label entries. Most teachers find it useful to put the date at the top of the page and to include a heading such as 'daily journal notes', 'reactions to teaching', 'reflections on child/lesson/collegial interaction'. This makes it easy to locate previous entries and lends coherence to the writing.

Writing as a tool for self-understanding

This is perhaps the most challenging use of writing, and in fact, many of the previously mentioned problems are related to it. It is an uncomfortable process. It is hard for us to give up the comfort of some of our cherished ideas—to look at teaching in new ways, but it is also exhilarating. And, it is this ability to learn from practice that makes teaching professional. As we become aware of the complexity of teaching, it becomes easier to detach ourselves from it in order to learn from it. Our teaching becomes not 'good' or 'bad' but part of an ongoing process in a context of interacting elements, some of which are beyond our control and some that are within it. We know more about our classrooms and our teaching than anyone else does, and through reflective writing and collegial discussion, we have many opportunities to be architects of our own improvement.

Collegial discussion

There are several reasons for discussing some of your thoughts and feelings with your colleagues. For one thing, they will probably be curious about what you are doing. For another, they can act as a sounding-board for your ideas, both as professionals who are able to provide you with multiple perspectives and as friends who can listen and provide comments and suggestions empathetically. Bring to them a few of your dilemmas and concerns. Share selected pieces of your writing and ask for their reactions. Not only will you be learning from them, but you will be contributing to their professional development.

Learning from your writing

> Oh yes, I've enjoyed reading the past year's diary, and shall keep it up. I'm amused to find how its grown a person, with almost a face of its own.
>
> V. WOOLF's Diary, 28 December, 1919

There are many ways to learn from journal writing. The process of writing is educational. We have seen that it can be therapeutic (diary). Writing in a factual manner (log) can be useful in reconstructing experience, and it can be helpful in anaylsis and evaluation. Writing descriptively can provide insights and new awarenesses. Writing expressively and creatively can be exhilarating. Keeping a personal–professional journal incorporates these and other types of writing. It carries the implicit plan to return to the writing and to learn from it.

Returning to read the writing might, at first, provoke some anxiety. After all, we expose ourselves to the scrutiny of an observer. Whereas so much inter-personal communication is softened, even distorted (often to ensure social acceptance), journal writing as we have described it becomes authentic conversation with oneself, conversation that becomes increasingly congruent with inner thoughts. Learning from writing necessitates openness and curiosity, or as a teacher once said, 'listening with a quiet heart'.

Return to your writing. Sometimes you might wish to read over what you have written shortly after you have written it. Be careful not to judge it. Read it as you might a story or newspaper article of interest. Return to your writing whenever the interest occurs, perhaps weekly, bi-weekly, or monthly. Look in on the new faces you've grown; the new concerns and questions.

As you return to your writing, record your reactions and additional thoughts. You can clarify ideas and experiences as you reflect on them. Some teachers find it helpful to record their reactions in another colour in the margins. I date my comments so that when I return to them I can see what I have written at different times. It is like having a conversation with two or three people! And, in fact, it is.

As you peruse your journal, what thoughts, ideas, feelings, and reactions do you have.

- What main themes run through your writing? What questions?
- What do you write about? Do the topics change over time?
- Do you find 'philosophical' writing at times, and 'practical' writing at others?

- When do you record thoughts and feelings about teaching, and when do you write descriptively about students? Which students?
- What differences do you find in the style of your writing? How might you characterise your writing? The types of writing?
- When do you enjoy reading the writing? Do you sometimes have to coax yourself to read your journal entries? If so, when? Why?
- What does your writing tell you about teaching? About professional development? About schooling?
- Do you see patterns in your writing? If so, what are they?
- What does your handwriting suggest to you? What of the pressure you put on the pencil or pen? The speed with which you write? Do these vary? If so, why?
- What does your writing tell you about what you value? The challenges you face as a teacher?

As you read and re-read your journal, relax, follow your senses and appreciate the journey—rough parts and smooth. Experience the story as it unfolds and evolves. Share the cryptic nature of growth with Sybylla as she too explores the personal, life-long, and changing images of 'truth':

> This tale's as true as true can be,
> For what is truth or lies?
> So often much that's told by me
> When seen through other eyes,
> Becomes thereby unlike so much
> These others tell to you,
> And if things be the same as such,
> What is a scribe to do?
> Why, tell his tale of course, my friend,
> Or hold his tongue for aye,
> Or wait till fictive matters mend,
> Which may be by-and-bye.
> So here's a tale of things a-near
> That you may read and lend
> Without a fear—you'll need no tear—
> It hasn't any end.

(Franklin 1946, p. 9)

Appendix

Project abstract

Teacher reflections on classroom life: An empirical base for professional development*
Mary Louise Holly, Early Childhood Education, Kent State University

The current study is designed to add to the knowledge bases of teaching and professional development. It is a phenomenological study of the classroom teacher and a group of seven teachers who are reflecting upon, writing about, and discussing their lives in classrooms over a one-year period. Teachers keep written diaries which contain their thoughts on daily events, and serve as topics for discussion at weekly seminar sessions on teaching and professional development. Biweekly observations in each classroom are made by the researcher. Teachers were selected from seven school districts within a thirty-mile radius of Kent State University and include classroom levels from kindergarten through grade three in urban, rural, and suburban settings.

The research is built upon a conceptual framework which was generated in a previous study of teacher perceptions of professional growth and a perceptual approach to development (Holly 1977).

Major questions which are addressed include the following.

1. What do teachers think about on a daily and weekly basis? What are their problems and joys?
2. What are the events, interactions, and characteristics of the setting which have a significant impact upon their teaching and learning?
3. To what extent do activities and courses which are planned to assist them in their teaching actually help them?
4. What happens when teachers consciously reflect upon their teaching?
5. How do teachers help other teachers?
6. What do responses to these questions suggest for the improvement of support systems for professional development?

Data sources include diaries, transcriptions of seminar sessions, slides of each classroom and school, observations of participants' teaching and field notes, and informal interviews in each school (principals, children, parents, and staff members).

The phenomenological approach taken is one designed to enable the researcher to look at the classroom life of teachers from their perspectives and to describe the everyday and cululative experiences which affect their and their students' lives in classrooms (Edelfelt 1980).

*Project funded by the National Institute of Education

References

Ashton-Warner, S. (1973), *Teacher*, Bantam Books, New York.

Burke, M. L. (1983), 'A yoga perspective on time management', *Yoga Journal* (52), 40–1.

Bussis, A., Amarel, M., & Chittenden, E. (1975), *Beyond Surface Curriculum: An Interview Study of Teachers' Understandings*, Westview Press, Boulder, Colo.

Calkins, L. M. (1986), *The Art of Teaching Writing*, Heinemann, Portsmouth.

Combs, A. W., & Snygg, D. (1959), *Individual Behavior: A Perceptual Approach to Behavior*, rev. edn, Harper & Row, New York.

Combs, A., Avila, D., & Purkey, W. (1971), *Helping Relationships*, Allyn & Bacon, Boston.

Cummings, E. E. (1962), *A Selection of Poems 1923–1954*, Harcourt, Brace & World, New York.

Darwin, C. (1877), 'A biographical sketch of an infant', *Mind* 2, 296–94.

Dickens, C. (1917), *David Copperfield*, Collier & Son, New York (or Oxford University Press, New York, 1981).

Ebutt, D. (1985), 'Educational action research: Some general concerns and specific quibbles', in R. G. Burgess (ed.), *Issues in Educational Research: Qualitative Methods*, Falmer, Barcombe, Sussex.

Eisner, E. W. (1979), *The Educational Imagination: On the Design and Evaluation of School Programs*, Macmillan, New York.

Elkind, D. (1981), *The Hurried Child: Growing Up Too Fast Too Soon*, Addison-Wesley, Reading, Mass.

Erikson, E. (1975), *Life History and the Historical Moment*, Norton, New York.

Frank, A. (1952), *Anne Frank: The Diary of a Young Girl*, Doubleday, New York.

Franklin, M. (1901), *My Brilliant Career*, Georgian House, Melbourne.

Franklin, M. (1946), *My Career Goes Bung*, Georgian House, Melbourne.

Greene, M. (1978), *Landscapes of Learning*, Teachers' College Press, Columbia University, New York.

Greene, M. (1982), A general education curriculum: Retrospect and prospect—a viewing. Paper presented at the American Educational Research Association Annual Conference, New York.

Hammarskjold, D. (1964), *Markings*, Knopf, New York.

Holly, M. L. (1977), A conceptual framework for personal–professional growth: Implications for inservice education. Doctoral Dissertation, Michigan State University.

Holly, M. L. (1983a), Teacher reflections on classroom life: An empirical base for professional development. Progress Report to the National Institute of Education, Knowledge Use and School Improvement, Educational Research and Practice Unit.

Holly, M. L. (1983b), 'Teacher reflections on classroom life: Collaboration and professional development', *Australian Administrator* 4 (4), 1–4.

Holly, M. L., & Holly, B. P. (1983), 'Toward an empirically grounded conceptualization of staff development: Reflections on professional development in Cambridge and Liverpool, England', *Urban Educator* 7 (1), 75–87.

Hunt, D. (1978), 'Teacher personality, teacher attitude and teacher behavior', in B. Joyce, M. Brown & L. Peck (eds), *Flexibility in Teaching*, McCutcheon, Berkeley, Calif.

Jackson, P. (1971), 'Old dogs, new tricks', in L. J. Rubin (ed.), *Improving Inservice Education: Proposals and Procedures for Change*, Allyn and Bacon, Boston.

Jersild, A. (1955), *When Teachers Face Themselves*, Bureau of Publications, Teachers College, Columbia University, New York.

Kelley, E.C. (1947), *Education For What Is Real*, Harper, New York.

Kipling, P. (1930), 'Baa baa black sheep', in R. Jarrell (ed.), *The Best Short Stories of Kipling*, Hanover House, Garden City, New York.

Knowles, M. (1978), *The Adult Learner: A Neglected Species 1966*, 2nd edn, Gulf Publishing, Houston.

Kuhn, T. (1962), *The Structure of Scientific Revolutions*, University of Chicago Press, Chicago.

Lightfoot, S. L. (1983), *The Good High School: Portraits of Character and Culture*, Basic Books, New York.

Mallon, T. (1984), *A Book of One's Own: People and Their Diaries*, Ticknor & Fields, New York.

Markham, E. (1960), 'A creed', in *Poetry For Pleasure: The Hallmark Book of Poetry*, Doubleday, New York.

Maslow, A. (1979), *The Journals of A. H. Maslow*, Brooks/Cole, Monterey, Calif.

Merriam-Webster Dictionary (1974), Pocket Books, New York.

Nias, J. (1983), Learning and acting the role: In-school support for primary teachers. Paper presented at the American Educational Research Association Conference, Montreal.

Papalia, D., & Olds, S. W. (1975), *A Child's World: Infancy Through Adolescence*, McGraw Hill, New York, 12–13.

Pepys, S. (1893), *The Diary of Samuel Pepys*, Vols I & II, ed. H. B. Wheatley, Random House, New York.

Percy, W. (1980), *The Moviegoer*, Avon Books, New York.

Piaget, J. (1952), *The Origin of Intelligence in Children*, International Universities Press, New York.

Progoff, I. (1975), *At a Journal Workshop*, Dialogue House, New York.

Shutz, A. (1967), 'On multiple realities', in M. Natanson (ed.), *The Problem of Social Reality*, Collected Papers I, Martinus Nijhoff, The Hague, 209–12.

Simons, G. F. (1978), *Keeping Your Personal Journal*, Paulist Press, New York.

Smyth, W. J. (1984), *Clinical Supervision—Collaborative Learning About*

Teaching: A Handbook (EED 790 Instructional Supervision, ESA 843 School-Based Professional Development), Deakin University, Vic.

Sprinthall, N., & Sprinthall, L. (1980), 'Adult development and leadership training for mainstream education', in D. Corrigan & K. Howey (eds), *Concepts to Guide the Education of Experienced Teachers*, Council for Exceptional Children, Reston, Va.

Sprinthall, N., & Sprinthall, L. (1983), 'The teacher as an adult learner: A cognitive-developmental view', in G. Griffin (ed.), *Staff Development: Eighty-second Yearbook of the National Society for the Study of Education*, University of Chicago Press, Chicago.

Watts, A. W. (1951), *The Wisdom of Insecurity: A Message for an Age of Anxiety*, Pantheon, New York.

Woolf, V. (1953), *A Writer's Diary*, Hogarth, London.

Vance, V. S., & Schlechty, P. C. (1982), 'The distribution of academic ability in the teaching force: Policy implications', *Phi Delta Kappan* **64** (1).

Recommended reading

On writing and journal keeping

P. Abbs, *Autobiography in Education: An Introduction to the Subjective Discipline of Autobiography and its Central Place in the Education of Teachers*, Heinemann Educational Books, London, 1974.

M. Armstrong, *Closely Observed Children: Diary of a Primary Classroom*, Writers and Readers Pub., London, 1981.

M. M. Clay, *What Did I Write?*, Heineman Educational Books, Auckland, New Zealand, 1975.

Sister T. Craig, 'Self-discovery through writing personal journals', *Language Arts*, vol. 60, no. 3, March 1983, pp. 373–9.

L. Daniel, *How to Write Your Own Life Story: A Step by Step Guide for the Non-Professional Writer*, Chicago Review Press, Chicago, 1985.

J. Fleming, *His Affair*, M. Evans, New York, 1976.

M. Franklin, *My Brilliant Career*, Georgian House, Melbourne, 1901.

M. Franklin, *My Career Goes Bung*, Angus & Robertson, Sydney, 1946.

M. Franklin, *Childhood at Brindabella: My First Ten Years*, Angus & Robertson, Sydney, 1963.

D. H. Graves, *Writing: Teachers and Children at Work*, Heineman Educational Books, Exeter, NH, 1983.

G. Greene, *A Sort of Life*, Pocket Books, New York, 1972.

M. L. Holly, *Writing to Grow: Keeping a Personal–Professional Journal*, Heinemann, Portsmouth, 1987.

R. Kaiser, 'The way of the journal', *Psychology Today*, March 1981, pp. 64–76.

R. Kanin, *Write the Story of Your Life*, Hawthorn/Dutton, New York, 1981.

S. Kopp, *If You Meet the Buddha on the Way, Kill Him*, Science and Behavior Books, Palo Alto, Calif., 1972.

'Learning to write: An expression of language', Special Topic of *Theory Into Practice*, vol. 19, no. 3, Summer 1980.

K. Macrorie, *Searching Writing*, Upper Montclair, Boynton/Cook, 1984.

T. Mallon, *A Book of One's Own: People and Their Diaries*, Ticknor & Fields, New York, 1984.

M. J. Moffit, & C. Painter (eds), *Revelations: Diaries of Women*, Random House, New York, 1974.

I. Progoff, *At a Journal Workshop*, Dialogue House, New York, 1975.
B. Provost, *Make Every Word Count*, Writers' Digest Books, Cincinnati, Ohio, 1980.
W. M. Runyan, *Life Histories and Psychobiography: Explorations in Theory and Method*, Oxford University Press, New York, 1982.
G. Simon, *Keeping Your Personal Journal*, Paulist Press, Toronto, 1978.
R. D. Walshe, *Donald Graves in Australia: Children Want to Write*, Bridge Printery, Roseberry, NSW, 1981.
E. Welty, *One Writer's Beginnings*, Harvard University Press, Cambridge, Mass., 1984.
R. Zinsser, *On Writing Well: An Informal Guide to Writing Nonfiction*, 3rd edn, Harper & Row, New York, 1985.

On teaching and professional development

M. Armstrong, *Closely Observed Children: Diary of a Primary Classroom*, Writers and Readers, London, 1980.
S. Ashton-Warner, *Teacher*, Bantam Books, New York, 1973.
S. J. Ball & I. F. Goodson, *Teachers' Lives and Careers*, Falmer, Barcombe, Sussex, 1985.
A. Bussis, M. Amarel & E. Chittendon, *Beyond Surface Curriculum: An Interview Study of Teachers' Understandings*, Westview Press, Boulder, Calif., 1975.
D. Elkind, *The Hurried Child: Growing Up Too Fast Too Soon*, Addison-Wesley, Reading, Mass., 1981.
M. Greene, *Teacher as Stranger*, Teachers College Press, Columbia University, New York, 1973.
M. Greene, *Landscapes of Learning*, Teachers College Press, Columbia University, New York, 1978.
P. W. Jackson, *Life in Classrooms*, Holt, Rinehart & Winston, New York, 1968.
P. W. Jackson, *The Practice of Teaching*, Teachers College Press, New York, 1986.
A. Jersild, *When Teachers Face Themselves*, Teachers College Press, Columbia University, New York, 1955.
E. C. Kelley, *Education For What is Real*, Harper, New York, 1947.
P. Knoblock & A. P. Golstein, *The Lonely Teacher*, Allyn & Bacon, Boston, 1971.
S. Kopp, *Even a Stone Can Be a Teacher: Learning and Growing from the Experiences of Everyday Life*, Houghton Mifflin, Boston, 1985.
J. Rudduck & D. Hopkins, *Research as a Basis for Teaching: Readings from the Work of Lawrence Stenhouse*, Heinemann, London, 1985.
D. Schön, *The Reflective Practictioner: How Professionals Think in Action*, Basic Books, New York, 1983.
W. J. Smyth, *Reflection-in-Action* (EED 432 Educational Leadership in Schools), Vic., 1986.
L. Stenhouse, *An Introduction to Curriculum Research and Development*, Heinemann, London, 1975.
A. R. Tom, *Teaching as a Moral Craft*, Longman, New York, 1984.